GW01401466

Original title:
Happiness Guide

Author: Clement Portlander
ISBN HARDBACK: 978-9916-88-244-3
ISBN PAPERBACK: 978-9916-88-245-0

The Canvas of Cheer

Brush strokes of yellow,
Dancing on the white,
Happiness in colors,
Brightening the night.

Every smile a canvas,
Painted with delight,
Every laugh a brushstroke,
Filling hearts with light.

Joy is the palette,
Mixing shades of hope,
In this vibrant vision,
Together we all cope.

With every brush we share,
Life's beauty we reveal,
In this canvas of cheer,
Love is the ideal.

Shadows of Laughter

In the corners linger,
Echoes of our play,
Shadows stretching longer,
As the light fades away.

Whispers in the twilight,
Tales of days gone by,
Laughter as our beacon,
As time softly flies.

Every giggle captures,
Moments we hold dear,
In the shadows dancing,
There's nothing we must fear.

In the heart of twilight,
Where memories surround,
Laughter leads us onward,
In joy we are found.

The Joyful Journey

Step by step we wander,
On this road of dreams,
With laughter as our compass,
And sunlight's warming gleams.

Every path together,
Each moment we embrace,
With joy as our guide,
We find our rightful place.

We sail through the valleys,
Climb mountains high and far,
In the journey of the heart,
Together where we are.

With every heartbeat's rhythm,
And every smile we share,
The joy of our journey,
Is found everywhere.

Finding Sunbeams

In the morning light we rise,
Chasing whispers of the skies.
Through the leaves, the shadows play,
Finding sunbeams, bright and gay.

Golden rays upon our skin,
Where the warmth of hope begins.
Every sigh, a gentle peace,
In this moment, we release.

Embracing the Brightness

Brush of light upon our cheeks,
In the glow, the spirit speaks.
Hearts ignited by the flame,
Embracing joy, it's not the same.

Every laugh, a song we share,
In the warmth, we shed our care.
Hand in hand, through fields we roam,
In this brightness, we find home.

Whispers of Delight

Gentle winds that softly sway,
Carry dreams that gently play.
In the hush, a secret sound,
Whispers of delight abound.

Laughter dances on the breeze,
Filling hearts with perfect ease.
Moments cherished, time stands still,
In this joy, we find our will.

The Path to Serene Smiles

Upon the trail where blossoms grow,
We wander free, our spirits flow.
Every step, a breath of grace,
The path to smiles we embrace.

In the distance, laughter chimes,
Echoing through the sands of time.
Together, we'll forever stay,
On this journey, come what may.

Mosaic of Joyful Memories

Fragments of laughter, bright and clear,
Moments we cherish, held so dear.
Colors of friendship, woven tight,
In this mosaic, we find our light.

Each smile a tile, vibrant and bold,
Stories of warmth, gently told.
With every memory, our hearts entwine,
A canvas of joy, forever divine.

Ladders to Laughter

Climbing up high, we chase the fun,
Each step a giggle, a race we run.
Rungs made of joy, painted so bright,
Reaching new heights, filled with delight.

At the top, we see the view,
Laughter surrounds, fresh and new.
From this peak, we share our dreams,
Together we shine, like sunlit beams.

A Tapestry of Grins

Threads of laughter, woven with grace,
In every stitch, a warm embrace.
Patterns of joy, rich and grand,
A tapestry woven, hand in hand.

Each smile a color, each giggle a thread,
Together we weave, love widespread.
In life's design, we find our place,
A beautiful work, a timeless space.

Rays of Optimism

Light breaking through on a cloudy day,
Hope shining bright, showing the way.
With every ray, our spirits rise,
Chasing the shadows, reaching the skies.

In this golden glow, we find our dream,
A future of promise, a radiant beam.
Together we'll dance, hearts open wide,
With rays of optimism, side by side.

Joyful Compass

In the heart, a compass gleams,
Guiding us through hopeful dreams.
With every smile, we chart our way,
In joy's embrace, we choose to stay.

Waves of laughter fill the air,
Moments cherished, free from care.
Together we sail, hand in hand,
Adventures waiting, oh so grand.

The sun sets low, painting the sky,
With colors bright that catch the eye.
In the twilight, we find our grace,
With joy as our guide, we'll find our place.

The Path to Serene Smiles

Softly glows the morning light,
Awakening dreams, pure and bright.
We walk the path with gentle ease,
Finding joy in rustling leaves.

With every step, a smile blooms,
Chasing shadows, dispelling glooms.
In laughter shared, we take a stand,
Together in this joyful land.

The heart sings sweet, a melody,
Echoes of love, wild and free.
In the stillness, peace we find,
A tapestry of souls entwined.

Embracing Sunlight Within

Golden rays of warmth descend,
Whispers of love, on us depend.
With open arms, we greet the day,
In sunlight's hug, we laugh and play.

Shadows vanish, fears take flight,
As we bask in pure delight.
With every heartbeat, joy will spin,
A dance of light that lies within.

Together we weave our dreams so bright,
Painting the world with love's pure light.
In this embrace, we find our home,
Through every step, we are not alone.

Whispers of Contentment

Softly sings the evening breeze,
Carrying secrets among the trees.
In gentle tones, the world unfolds,
As twilight whispers stories told.

With every star, a wish ignites,
Guiding hearts through quiet nights.
Contentment lingers in the air,
A sacred bond we choose to share.

In stillness found, we breathe with ease,
Wrapped in love, like autumn leaves.
Each moment ripe with endless grace,
Whispers of joy, our hearts embrace.

The Echo of Happy Moments

In the garden, laughter sways,
Memories dance in golden rays.
Echoes of joy fill the air,
Whispers of love everywhere.

Time stands still in cherished sights,
Each heartbeat glows with pure delights.
A tapestry of smiles unveiled,
Through every tale, joy has sailed.

Sunset hues kiss the day goodbye,
As stars twinkle high in the sky.
Each moment cherished, held so tight,
In the echoes, hearts take flight.

Through the years, a gentle song,
In every moment, we belong.
Together woven, bright and bold,
The echo of memories never old.

Soaring with Joy

Above the clouds, our spirits rise,
With open hearts, we touch the skies.
Wings of laughter lift us high,
In a dance of glee, we fly.

Beneath the sun, we find our grace,
Joyful energy fills the space.
With every heartbeat, freedom sings,
In the air, our spirit flings.

Through valleys deep and mountains tall,
We chase the echoes, hear the call.
With every step, our hearts ignite,
Guided by joy, we take flight.

Hand in hand, we chase the breeze,
Dancing with leaves on swaying trees.
Soaring in joy, we embrace the day,
In this moment, we choose to stay.

Unwritten Pages of Laughter

In a book that has no end,
Each chapter holds joy to blend.
Pages blank await the spark,
In laughter's light, we leave our mark.

Tales of funny mishaps arise,
Every giggle holds surprise.
With each new line, our hearts collide,
In this story, we confide.

Footsteps echo down the lane,
Memories woven in sunshine rain.
Together we craft each new line,
In unwritten pages, our hearts shine.

With laughter as our guiding star,
We navigate near and far.
The canvas blank, our dreams expand,
In laughter's embrace, we take a stand.

The Fusion of Joy and Gratitude

Under the sun, we gather near,
Hearts aligned with love and cheer.
Grateful whispers fill the air,
A fusion of joy, beyond compare.

Every moment, a gift we hold,
Stories shared, both new and old.
In every smile, a spark ignites,
Illuminating our hearts' delights.

Together we rise, hand in hand,
In this journey, we understand.
Thankful hearts and joyful song,
In this unity, we all belong.

With every breath, we celebrate,
Life's sweet moments never late.
The fusion of joy and gratitude,
Creates a world of endless food.

Conversations with Light

In the morning glow, we meet,
Whispers of dawn, soft and sweet.
Shadows retreat with each ray,
Painting the world in bright array.

Light dances on the leaves above,
A gentle chat, a song of love.
Each flicker tells a tale anew,
In vibrant hues, the day breaks through.

Through shimmering beams, pathways gleam,
Illuminating every dream.
Chasing the dark, we find our way,
In the warmth of light, we choose to stay.

At twilight's edge, we pause and breathe,
Conversations soar, our hearts believe.
In the fading glow, secrets unfold,
With light as our guide, a story told.

Veils of Cheer

In every laugh, a shroud of light,
Veils of cheer dance in the night.
Bringing joy to weary hearts,
In simple moments, happiness starts.

Beneath the stars, we gather close,
Sharing stories, a vibrant dose.
Each smile, a bridge, spanning the gap,
Woven in warmth, like a cozy lap.

With every hug, our spirits rise,
Veils of cheer reflected in our eyes.
In friendship's embrace, we find our zest,
United in laughter, we are blessed.

As dawn approaches, hope is clear,
With every breath, we hold what's dear.
Veils of cheer, like petals fall,
Embracing the world, we answer the call.

Unfolding Smiles

Like flowers blooming in the sun,
Unfolding smiles, a joy begun.
Each petal tells a story bright,
In the garden of warmth and light.

With every glance, connections grow,
In silent words, our feelings flow.
A gentle nod, a warm embrace,
Unfolding smiles, love finds its place.

Through trials faced, we stand as one,
Hand in hand, our journey's fun.
In laughter shared, our worries flee,
Unfolding smiles, forever free.

As twilight casts a golden hue,
With every heartbeat, we renew.
A world transformed with every grin,
Unfolding smiles, let life begin.

Windows to Blissful Days

Peering through panes of light and hue,
Windows to blissful days, fresh and true.
Each glimpse, a memory finely framed,\nIn colors bright,
our lives are named.

The laughter shared behind closed doors,
Echoes of joy, like gentle roars.
Every moment framed with grace,
Windows open, our hearts embrace.

As seasons shift, the views may change,
Yet love's reflection will never range.
In every day, a story stays,
Windows to blissful, endless ways.

So let us gaze with eager hearts,
Discovering magic life imparts.
Through windows wide, our spirits soar,
Blissful days await, forevermore.

The Symphony of Smiles

In the morning light we shine,
With laughter twinkling in our eyes.
Each smile a note, a sweet design,
Creating magic, a joyful surprise.

Harmony found in every laugh,
Echoing soft in the gentle breeze.
Laughter brings joy, like a photograph,
Memories form, our hearts at ease.

Together we dance through the day,
As melodies lead us on our way.
In this symphony, we find our place,
In every smile, a warm embrace.

A Map to Cheerful Encounters

Life unfolds like a treasure map,
Each smile a mark, a sacred spot.
We wander through fields, share a laugh,
Connecting moments that can't be forgot.

Paths of sunshine and whispers sweet,
Guiding us to friends we meet.
With open hearts, we discover grace,
In every smile, we find our space.

A map drawn with kindness, open wide,
Inviting all to share the ride.
Through cheerful encounters, we explore,
A world of joy, forever in store.

The Dance of Lively Spirits

Under the moonlight, spirits swirl,
A dance of joy, a vibrant twirl.
With every step, laughter ignites,
Creating warmth on these cool nights.

Hands held high, we sway as one,
In this lively dance, all worries shun.
With rhythm flowing, we celebrate,
The magic found in moments great.

Each spin and leap, a heart set free,
In this joyous dance, we find our glee.
Lively spirits, bright and clear,
In every move, we draw you near.

Gentle Puffs of Joy

Softly floating on a breeze,
Gentle puffs of joy appear.
Whispers of laughter through the trees,
Filling our hearts with warmth and cheer.

Like feathers drifting, light and free,
They dance around, a sweet delight.
In playful whispers, joy agrees,
Creating moments, pure and bright.

In every heartbeat, in every sigh,
Gentle puffs of joy unfold.
A simple touch, a soft reply,
In every story, love is told.

Unraveling Blissful Secrets

In shadows deep, whispers play,
A gentle breeze where dreams sway.
Secrets dance in twilight's glow,
Revealing truth we long to know.

Fingers trace the hidden signs,
In rustling leaves the heart aligns.
Moments paused, the world in hush,
In silence blooms the sweetened rush.

With every breath, a story told,
In laughter shared, in arms we hold.
Unlock the door to what resides,
In blissful realms where love abides.

So let us walk, hand in hand,
Through softest paths, on golden sand.
Unraveling secrets that we keep,
In this embrace, our souls shall leap.

Tides of Cheer

The sun dips low, a glimmer bright,
Awakening the joyful night.
Ocean waves in rhythmic dance,
Invite our hearts to take a chance.

Laughter rings like silver bells,
In every tide, a story dwells.
Chasing dreams along the shore,
We find the happiness we adore.

With every splash, the world feels new,
A canvas painted with every hue.
Seas of cheer, we ebb and flow,
In perfect moments, time's soft glow.

Together we create a song,
In every heart, where we belong.
Tides of joy that never cease,
In waves of love, we find our peace.

The Color of Joy

Painted skies in morning light,
Burst of colors, pure delight.
A canvas stretched with dreams untold,
In every shade, a heart of gold.

Crimson blush of passion's flare,
Dancing quiet in the air.
Emerald fields where laughter grows,
In every step, the joy bestows.

Golden rays embrace the day,
Whispering secrets of the play.
Each hue a note, a melody,
In vibrant breaths, we all are free.

So let us blend in love's bright art,
With every stroke, we share our heart.
The color of joy in every scene,
A masterpiece in life's sweet glean.

Symphony of Light

The dawn unfolds with gentle grace,
A symphony of light we trace.
In every ray, a note resounds,
Uniting life, as beauty bounds.

The stars ignite the velvet night,
Each twinkle sings a song of light.
Moonlit whispers softly play,
Guiding dreams that drift away.

In every heartbeat, rhythms flow,
A harmony that all can know.
Together we create the sound,
Of love and joy that starves the ground.

So let us dance in this embrace,
With every soul, a sacred space.
In the symphony where we belong,
We are the light, we are the song.

Recipes for a Grateful Soul

A pinch of laughter, a dash of care,
Mix in the memories we all share.
Stir with kindness, let love unfold,
Serve with gratitude, a treasure more than gold.

Embrace each moment, let worries cease,
Find joy in giving, a path to peace.
Sprinkle in hope like seeds in spring,
Taste the delight that gratefulness can bring.

Gather the stories that shape our days,
Crafting connections in countless ways.
A recipe simple yet rich and deep,
For a grateful soul, the heart's gentle sweep.

Crafting Joyful Echoes

Whispers of laughter dance in the air,
Every moment a treasure, precious and rare.
With each shared smile, life's canvas we paint,
Creating echoes where hearts grow faint.

Threads of connection woven with love,
Bright flashes of joy that rise above.
Found in the silence, the softest of sounds,
Joyful echoes in the space that surrounds.

Through shared stories, our spirits take flight,
Crafting a tapestry woven with light.
In every encounter, a spark to ignite,
Echoes of joy that linger, just right.

The Gentle Breeze of Bliss

Softly it whispers, a gentle embrace,
Carrying whispers from a tranquil place.
It dances through leaves, in sunlight it plays,
A serenade sweet on warm summer days.

With every breath, let the calmness unfold,
Inviting the warmth as the stories are told.
Cradled in moments where laughter flows free,
The gentle breeze, where our spirits can be.

In quiet reflections, it stirs up delight,
A soothing reminder of love's pure light.
Guiding us softly to where we belong,
The gentle breeze, like a soft, vibrant song.

Colors of a Joyful Journey

A canvas of laughter, hues bold and bright,
Every step painted in pure delight.
Brushstrokes of friendship shade our way,
Coloring moments in a vibrant display.

Golden sunrises greet the dawn,
While azure skies cheer as we move on.
Rays of warm sunshine, deep emerald leaves,
In nature's palette, our heart believes.

With every twist and turn that we tread,
We gather the colors where memories spread.
An artful journey, a story to tell,
Living in colors that capture us well.

Threads of Cheerful Days

In the morning, sunlight beams,
Waking dreams of softest schemes.
Laughter dances on the breeze,
Wrapping hearts with gentle ease.

Running through the fields of gold,
Every story, new and bold.
Chasing shadows, bright and free,
Life's a tapestry, you see.

Whispers of a joyful song,
Binding souls where we belong.
Hand in hand, we find our way,
Stitching moments, day by day.

As the twilight paints the sky,
Memories in hues comply.
Threads woven with love's fine art,
Keep the cheer within the heart.

Portraits of Bliss

Brushstrokes of a vibrant hue,
Capture dreams both old and new.
Every smile, a tale to tell,
In each canvas, joy does dwell.

Echoes of laughter fill the air,
Fleeting moments, light as air.
Days where time is held so still,
Crafting joy beyond the thrill.

Colors dance in perfect light,
The simplest things feel so right.
In this gallery of glee,
Every heart can feel so free.

Memories framed in love's embrace,
Cherished moments we can't replace.
With each brush, the heart will sing,
A portrait of the joy we bring.

Picking Daisies of Enjoyment

In the meadows, petals white,
Dancing softly in the light.
Each daisy holds a secret prayer,
Whispers of joy linger in the air.

We gather laughter, sweet and bright,
With every stem, a pure delight.
Moments stitched like flowers bloom,
Filling hearts with rich perfume.

Underneath the vast blue sky,
Time slows down, we breathe, we sigh.
With each pluck, a memory we make,
In this moment, the world we shake.

As the sun dips low and gold,
Our hearts wrap in stories told.
Picking daisies, we are free,
Joy found in simplicity.

Chasing the Light

The dawn breaks with a gentle sigh,
Painting the earth as colors fly.
We run wild where shadows play,
Chasing dreams that greet the day.

With every step, the world unfolds,
Stories written in the golds.
Footprints left upon the sand,
Memories made, hand in hand.

The sunset whispers, soft and low,
Bidding farewell, but here we grow.
Bound by laughter, love, and might,
Together, we are chasing light.

In the stars, our hopes ignite,
Guiding us through the endless night.
With hearts wide open, we will soar,
In this light, we seek for more.

Navigating the Seas of Merriment

Sailing on waves of laughter,
Tides of joy uplift our souls.
With every breeze, we gather cheer,
In this voyage, heartbeats roll.

Glimmers of sunlight kiss the waves,
As we dance on the vibrant tide.
Every splash, a burst of glee,
With friends by our side, we glide.

Anchored in moments, we find peace,
Treasures of friendship, pure and bright.
We chart our course through laughter's map,
In the night, our spirits take flight.

To navigate joy's boundless sea,
With the stars guiding our way.
May we always find our compass,
In each and every playful day.

The Essence of Grinning Hearts

In corners where smiles abound,
Hearts beat in joyous embrace.
With every glance, warmth is found,
In laughter, we leave our trace.

A gentle breeze whispers fun,
All worries drift far from sight.
Together, we shine like the sun,
With hearts grinning ever so bright.

Moments bloom in vibrant hues,
Each chuckle, a petal in time.
In a symphony of fond views,
We dance through life's joyful rhyme.

Here's to the essence we hold dear,
A testament to love's sweet art.
With every memory crystal clear,
In the canvas of grinning hearts.

Curating Moments of Joy

In the gallery of our days,
Every laughter is a frame.
Captured in joyous arrays,
Each second, a flicker of flame.

Curating smiles like fine art,
We paint with colors of mirth.
Every tick of the clock, a part,
Of the treasure we find on Earth.

Let the world fade in soft blur,
As we weave tales filled with glee.
Moments that never defer,
In this tapestry, we are free.

With every heartbeat, let's collect,
The shards of laughter that glow.
In this life, may we reflect,
On the joy that we choose to sow.

Letters to the Cheerful Spirit

Dear spirit of joy, we write you now,
With letters filled with light and cheer.
Each word, a gift, a solemn vow,
To cherish the moments we hold dear.

You dance in laughter, you leap in glee,
A muse that leads us along the way.
With you, dear spirit, we wander free,
In the sun's embrace, we joyfully play.

Through scribbled notes and whispered dreams,
Your essence fills the air we share.
In every smile, your magic beams,
An invitation to suspend our care.

So here's to you, our radiant muse,
With love penned deep within our hearts.
In every letter, joy's magic brews,
For in smiling souls, true art imparts.

Sunshine Through Raindrops

Tiny glimmers on the ground,
Nature's jewels all around.
A dance of light, a sweet surprise,
We find the joy in cloudy skies.

A soft embrace from sun's warm grace,
Colors bloom in every space.
Raindrops play a gentle tune,
While we dream beneath the moon.

Laughter echoes through the air,
Memories made without a care.
Hand in hand, we wander free,
Each moment's pure, just you and me.

Hold the magic, let it flow,
Love and light, in hearts we sow.
Sunshine glows through every tear,
A promise kept, forever near.

The Melody of a Joyful Heart

Soft whispers float on gentle breeze,
A harmony that brings us ease.
Tunes of laughter, sweet and clear,
In every note, we feel no fear.

Every smile, a vibrant chord,
In life's song, we are adored.
Together we create the sound,
A melody that knows no bound.

Radiant rhythms, spirits soar,
Dancing freely, wanting more.
Let the music guide our feet,
In this dance, our souls will meet.

Joyful hearts with voices strong,
In unity, we sing along.
Celebrate this life we share,
In every note, we find our prayer.

Radiance in Every Step

With each step, the world awakes,
A journey full of gentle stakes.
Sunlit paths beneath our feet,
In every turn, a story sweet.

The morning dew, a spark divine,
Guiding us through, your hand in mine.
Every moment, a treasure found,
In this dance, we feel unbound.

Whispers of love in every stride,
With you, I have nothing to hide.
Radiance glows in our embrace,
Together we find our place.

Beneath the stars, the journey's glow,
With every breath, the love will flow.
In every step, joy intertwines,
As we write our own designs.

Celebrating the Little Joys

A warm cup steaming in our hands,
Quiet mornings filled with plans.
Tender moments shared in light,
In simple things, our hearts take flight.

Laughter shared beneath the sun,
Every smile, a victory won.
We dance through life with open eyes,
Finding beauty as it flies.

The touch of grass beneath our toes,
In these moments, love just grows.
Starry nights and midnight talks,
In the silence, magic walks.

Let's gather joy in each small act,
In every word, a love compact.
Together, let's embrace the grace,
In little joys, we find our place.

Seeds of Serenity

In the quiet garden, dreams take root,
Gentle whispers float on the breeze,
Each seed a promise, pure and astute,
Nurtured by hope, growing with ease.

Sunlight dances on leaves so green,
Raindrops kiss the earth with grace,
In this haven, peace is seen,
Harmony finds its rightful place.

Time slows down, worries dissipate,
Nature's embrace, soothing and kind,
In the heart, love resonates,
A tranquil spirit intertwined.

So plant the seeds, let your heart be light,
For in stillness, joy will bloom,
A garden of bliss, radiant and bright,
In the silence, find your room.

Echoes of Laughter: A Journey

Through the valleys, laughter rings,
Echoes play upon the hills,
Childlike spirits, joy that clings,
Adventure calls, the heart it thrills.

In every step, stories unfold,
Moments captured in time's embrace,
With every smile, warmth takes hold,
Life's tapestry, a wondrous space.

We dance through storms, hand in hand,
Finding light in shadows cast,
Together we rise, like grains of sand,
The present lingers, holding fast.

As the journey weaves and bends,
Laughter echoes through the years,
In each heart, joy transcends,
Uniting us through smiles and tears.

The Palette of Positivity

With brushes dipped in vibrant hues,
We paint the world with hopes anew,
Colors bright, erasing blues,
A masterpiece in every view.

Strokes of kindness, wide and free,
Creating warmth where shadows play,
From every heart, a jubilee,
Together chasing gloom away.

In the canvas of our days,
Let laughter blend with endless cheer,
With every moment, spark the blaze,
Crafting a vision bright and clear.

So let us paint, unite our souls,
With positivity as our guide,
In this masterpiece, our essence rolls,
A colorful journey, side by side.

Illuminated by Kindness

In the twilight, hearts ignite,
Beacons shining through the night,
Acts of kindness, pure delight,
Guiding souls to what is right.

A simple word, a gentle touch,
Can lift the weary from their woe,
A little love means so much,
In kindness, we all grow.

Together we weave a radiant thread,
Stories shared in every glance,
In unity, no heart is misled,
As compassion leads our dance.

So let us shine, embrace the flame,
In our hearts, let kindness reign,
Bringing joy, and never shame,
Illuminated, we break the chain.

Crafting a Daydream

In the quiet of morning light,
Thoughts dance, taking flight.
Colors swirl in the mind's eye,
A canvas waiting to fly high.

Whispers of wishes softly collide,
On the gentle waves, we ride.
Each dream a step, a guiding star,
Leading us to where wonders are.

In silent corners, visions bloom,
Filling shadows with bright hues of gloom.
Crafting moments, spun with care,
In daydreams, we find our lair.

With every heartbeat, we create,
A world where hopes and dreams await.
In the fabric of dreams, we play,
Crafting a bright, eternal day.

Blossoms of Contentment

In the garden where shadows fall,
Gentle petals hear the call.
Whispers of joy in the breeze,
Blossoms sway with effortless ease.

Under skies of azure hue,
Nature paints a melody true.
With each bloom, a tale unfolds,
In their grace, a warmth enfolds.

Time slows down in fragrant lanes,
Where laughter dances and love remains.
Blossoms of joy, hearts intertwine,
In contentment's glow, we brightly shine.

In every petal's soft embrace,
We find solace and gentle grace.
In this moment, life's sweet tune,
We celebrate beneath the moon.

Illuminating the Mundane

In the early light of day,
Simple tasks come out to play.
A cup of warmth, steam rising high,
In stillness, the magic does lie.

The rustle of leaves, a soft sigh,
Glimmers of joy in a passerby.
Each footstep, a story to tell,
In the ordinary, we dwell well.

Through windowpanes, sunlight streams,
Awakening the world of dreams.
In mundane moments, we find our art,
Illuminating life's tender heart.

From bustling streets to quiet nooks,
There's beauty in familiar hooks.
In every glance and gentle touch,
The mundane holds so very much.

The Spirit of Playfulness

With laughter ringing through the air,
We dance and spin without a care.
The spirit of play, a joyful spark,
Illuminates the world so dark.

Chasing shadows, running free,
Imagination's wild decree.
In every game, a tale we weave,
In the heart of joy, we believe.

Swinging high on laughter's wings,
In the chorus of joy, everyone sings.
Exploring paths with childlike glee,
The spirit of play sets us free.

With every smile, a bridge is built,
In moments of fun, there's no guilt.
In the spirit of play, we unite,
As one bright star, we light the night.

Treasures of a Joyful Mind

In gardens where the smiles bloom bright,
Thoughts take wing like birds in flight.
Moments cherished, laughter shared,
In joyful hearts, love is declared.

A sunbeam dances on the floor,
Whispers of peace, the spirit soars.
Each memory a gem, each friend a star,
Together we shine, near and far.

In small joys, we find our gold,
Stories of hope in hearts retold.
A treasure map of every cheer,
Guiding us through the haze of fear.

Every heartbeat a precious find,
In the garden of a joyful mind.
We gather moments, we plant the seeds,
In the richness of love, our soul's needs.

Embracing the Gift of Today

Each dawn is painted with promise anew,
A canvas vast, with colors so true.
With open hearts, we greet the light,
Embracing each moment, taking flight.

The ticking clock, a gentle sound,
In each heartbeat, joy can be found.
Let gratitude fill the air we share,
In this fleeting time, let's truly care.

Today's the gift we hold so dear,
Breathe in the magic, let go of fear.
With every step, let us be bold,
Creating memories more precious than gold.

In laughter's echo, in love's embrace,
We weave our dreams in time and space.
So here's to today, and all it brings,
Embrace the gift, let your spirit sing.

Joy's Compass

A compass made of laughter bright,
Guides us through the darkest night.
With every smile, a new direction,
In joy we find our pure connection.

Through paths of trials, over hills we roam,
With joy as our guide, we're never alone.
In every heartbeat, in every cheer,
The compass points to love, so dear.

In storms of doubt, when shadows creep,
We hold our joy, a treasure to keep.
Navigating life with gratitude's tune,
Our hearts aligned beneath the moon.

So let joy lead our way each day,
A compass set for joyful play.
Through gentle turns and bends we find,
The beauty that lives in a joyful mind.

The Art of Laughter

In joyful bursts, laughter takes flight,
Painting the world in colors so bright.
A symphony of echoes, ringing clear,
Uniting our souls, drawing us near.

When shadows loom, and spirits fade,
Laughter becomes the sweet serenade.
A simple joke, a playful pun,
In every chuckle, we become one.

The art of laughter, a healing muse,
In moments of joy, we easily choose.
Together we stand, through thick and thin,
In laughter's embrace, we always win.

So let us laugh, let spirits soar,
In the art of laughter, we find the door.
To joy and light, a boundless art,
Forever in laughter, we play our part.

The Journey to Joyful Meadows

In fields of gold, we roam so free,
A breeze of laughter, you and me.
With sunlit paths that guide our way,
We'll chase the clouds and greet the day.

With every step, the heartbeats rise,
A symphony beneath the skies.
Through gentle streams, our spirits play,
Together we shall find our way.

Embracing dreams that life bestows,
In joyful meadows, friendship grows.
The whispers of the flowers greet,
A journey shared, so pure and sweet.

So let us wander, hand in hand,
Where timeless moments softly stand.
In joy's embrace, we'll forever stay,
In joyful meadows, come what may.

Stargazing on Days of Laughter

Beneath the stars, where dreams ignite,
We share our wishes, hearts take flight.
In the tapestry of night so grand,
We find our joy, hand in hand.

Laughter echoes through the trees,
Soft melodies carried by the breeze.
With every twinkle, stories unfold,
Of hope and love, both brave and bold.

Those gentle moments, pure and bright,
Illuminate our shared delight.
In starlit skies, our spirits twine,
In endless laughter, you're truly mine.

So let's embrace these nights so clear,
With every giggle, I hold you near.
In the cosmic dance, forever bound,
Stargazing on this joyful ground.

A Tapestry of Cheer

With threads of laughter, woven tight,
We stitch our hearts with pure delight.
In every color, in every seam,
A tapestry of love's sweet dream.

Through whispered tales and playful jest,
Together we rise, we are the best.
In vibrant hues our stories blend,
Crafting joy that will not end.

In cozy corners, shadows play,
We find our sunshine in the gray.
With each moment, we intertwine,
Creating cheer, you are mine.

So let us weave this joyful art,
With every stitch, we warm the heart.
In laughter's glow, our spirits cheer,
A tapestry of love we hold dear.

Navigating Life's Bright Corners

Through winding paths, we seek the light,
Navigating with hearts so bright.
In every turn, new wonders wait,
Together we embrace our fate.

With each brave step, the world unfolds,
Stories of dreams and hopes untold.
In joyful sighs, we chase the dawn,
With courage found, we carry on.

The corners bright, they call our name,
In every smile, the spark of flame.
With laughter shared, we light the way,
Navigating life's bright ballet.

So take my hand, let's journey far,
With every heartbeat, we raise the bar.
In life's embrace, our spirits soar,
Together we'll explore much more.

Effervescent Dreams

In twilight's glow, where wishes sway,
Bubbles rise in a dance of play.
Whispers of stars, a gentle stream,
Carrying hearts through effervescent dreams.

A canvas painted with hopes so bright,
Each stroke a moment, pure delight.
Floating softly on clouds of glee,
Finding magic in what we see.

With laughter light, we chase the night,
In every corner, sparks ignite.
Together we weave a story grand,
Hand in hand, our dreams expand.

As dawn approaches, colors blend,
A tapestry of joy won't end.
Awake we stand, our passions gleam,
Embracing life with effervescent dreams.

Savoring the Sweetness

In gardens full of blooms so rare,
The fragrance lingers in the air.
With each petal, a story told,
Savoring sweetness in shades of gold.

A sip of honey, a tender kiss,
Moments fleeting, wrapped in bliss.
Life's little treats, we cherish most,
In quiet corners, we raise a toast.

Fruits of labor, love, and care,
Glimmers of joy beyond compare.
With every bite, memories swell,
In the heart's pantry, stories dwell.

Savoring sweetness, hand in hand,
A journey through life's precious land.
Together we'll feast, hearts interlace,
In simple pleasures, we find our place.

Crafting Joyful Moments

With threads of laughter, we entwine,
Crafting moments that truly shine.
In playful brushstrokes, colors blend,
A tapestry where joys extend.

Time pauses soft, as smiles are drawn,
In shared glances, a brand-new dawn.
With simple gestures, love takes flight,
Crafting joy in the soft moonlight.

Each heartbeat echoes tales of old,
In memories cherished, love unfolds.
We gather pieces, stitch them tight,
Creating warmth in the chilly night.

Life's fleeting hours, we mark them sweet,
In every laughter, our hearts will meet.
Together we build, together we'll find,
Crafting joyful moments in heart and mind.

The Secret of Luminous Days

In quiet dawns, where shadows play,
The secret whispers, in hues of gray.
Morning dew glistens on green leaves,
A promise alive that the heart believes.

Sunlight dances on glimmering streams,
Filling the world with glittering dreams.
In every ray, a spark of grace,
Luminous days, a warm embrace.

Clouds may gather, storms may sway,
Yet hope remains through every fray.
The secret lies in love's sweet stay,
Guiding us through, come what may.

With every sunset, colors blaze,
Unveiling life's intricate maze.
In each moment, we find the way,
To unlock the secret of luminous days.

The Garden of Delight

In the garden bright, flowers bloom,
Colors dance in the afternoon.
Breezes whisper secrets sweet,
Nature's joy is a pure retreat.

Butterflies flutter with delight,
Stars twinkle through the night.
Every petal tells a tale,
In this haven, love prevails.

Roses blush, and daisies sway,
In the warmth of golden ray.
Each leaf sings in harmony,
A symphony of ecstasy.

Moments linger, joy unfurls,
In the garden, peace swirls.
A sanctuary of the heart,
Here, all worries drift apart.

Unfolding Smiles

With each sunrise, warmth ignites,
Bringing laughter, pure delights.
Joyful faces greet the day,
In the light, worries stay away.

Little moments spark the cheer,
A shared glance, a friend so near.
In this dance of hearts so free,
Unfolding smiles, tranquility.

Whispers soft in twilight glow,
Promises of love we sow.
Each gesture, simple and bright,
Creates a world, pure and right.

Together we weave dreams anew,
Every smile, a gentle hue.
In this space where kindness grows,
Unfolding smiles, the heart knows.

Journey to Tranquil Joy

Beyond the hills where silence reigns,
A path unfolds, where peace remains.
Gentle streams and skies so blue,
Whisper softly, guiding you.

Footsteps lead where shadows play,
In the quiet, find your way.
Nature cradles every sigh,
In its arms, let worries fly.

With each breath, the heart will soar,
To tranquil realms forevermore.
Mountains echo with sweet refrain,
In this journey, joy we gain.

Find the stillness, let it bloom,
In every corner, scents of perfume.
This peaceful quest, a treasure trove,
Journey to joy, where spirits rove.

The Melody of Elation

In the air, a tune takes flight,
Notes of joy dance in the light.
Harmonies weave through the trees,
In this song, hearts feel at ease.

Each chord strikes a blissful chord,
Lifting spirits, they afford.
Moments woven soft and bright,
Elation sings through day and night.

Rhythms pulse, a gentle beat,
In our hearts, the music's heat.
With every laugh, the world aligns,
A melody that brightly shines.

So let us join in sweet refrain,
In the chorus, lose the pain.
Together find the pure elation,
In this song, our celebration.

Explorations in Contentment

In quiet moments, stillness reigns,
A soft embrace where peace remains.
With gentle laughter, hearts unite,
In simple joys, the world feels right.

Beneath the stars, a whispered song,
Together here, we all belong.
The little things, they spark delight,
In every breath, the soul takes flight.

A stroll through fields, where flowers bloom,
The scent of earth dispels all gloom.
In nature's arms, we find our way,
Contentment grows with each warm ray.

As sun sets low, the sky alight,
We gather close, our hearts ignite.
In shared moments, life's bright thread,
Contentment found in all we've said.

Kaleidoscope of Kindness

In every smile, a world unfolds,
A tapestry of warmth that holds.
With gentle hands and open heart,
We weave together, never apart.

A word of comfort, a helping hand,
In kindness shared, we take a stand.
Each act of love, a vibrant hue,
In life's mosaic, I find you.

Through random deeds, we plant the seeds,
Of empathy, fulfilling needs.
In laughter's echo, joy does rise,
A kaleidoscope before our eyes.

Together we create the light,
With every spark, our spirits bright.
In kindness' glow, the world's embraced,
A symphony of love interlaced.

The Architecture of Glee

In dreams we build, with hope our guide,
A structure strong, where joy abides.
With laughter's echo, walls surround,
In every heart, true glee is found.

The beams of light shine through the day,
With every hug, we find our way.
A fortress bright, against all fears,
With joy as stone, we share our tears.

Through open doors, our spirits soar,
In every smile, we seek for more.
Let dance and song lead us along,
In this grand space, we all belong.

Within these walls, let laughter ring,
In unison, our voices sing.
The foundation strong in every way,
In glee we build, day after day.

Cherished Sips of Joy

In morning light, a cup I hold,
With fragrant warmth, my heart unfold.
Each sip, a moment pure and sweet,
In simple pleasures, life's retreat.

With friends around, we raise a glass,
To laughter shared, let moments pass.
A toast to dreams, both big and small,
In every sip, we cherish all.

As evening falls, the stars appear,
With every clink, I feel you near.
Together here, we sip with glee,
In cherished times, we just let be.

The flavors dance upon our tongues,
A symphony that calls us young.
In each embrace, our spirits fly,
With every sip, we touch the sky.

Radiance in Everyday Moments

In the morning light, a soft glow,
Coffee steam rises, gentle and slow.
A child's laughter, pure and bright,
Moments like these, fill hearts with delight.

A blooming flower by the door,
Nature's beauty we can't ignore.
Pages turning in the afternoon sun,
Simple pleasures that bring us fun.

Conversations shared, laughter's embrace,
Time spent together, a sacred space.
The warmth of love in every glance,
Life's little joys, a precious dance.

As daylight fades, stars start to gleam,
Chasing sunsets, living the dream.
In every heartbeat, find the grace,
Radiance shines in every place.

Dancing with the Clouds

Up above the world so high,
Whispers of dreams in the sky.
Cotton candies drift and sway,
Painting colors in the day.

Footprints left on gentle air,
Weightless wonders everywhere.
The sun dips low, a fiery hue,
Clouds embrace the evening blue.

Children chase the shadows fast,
Imaginations, vast and vast.
Laughter echoes, sweet and loud,
Join the dance, oh joyful crowd.

Every moment, a gentle flight,
Finding magic in the night.
Dancing with the clouds above,
Life's rhythm sings of peace and love.

The Bright Side Manual

When the skies seem gray and dim,
Look for glimmers, let hope brim.
Every frown that tries to cling,
Push it back, let your heart sing.

A morning smile, the day ignites,
Kindness shared, a heart that lights.
In the simplest of things, we find,
A treasure chest, pure and kind.

Count the blessings, big and small,
Lift each other, let love call.
In the darkest hours, be the spark,
Guiding souls through the stark.

When shadows loom and fears arise,
Keep your focus on the prize.
The bright side manual, within reach,
A reminder of the joy we teach.

Celebrating Small Wonders

A raindrop glistens on a leaf,
Nature's art, a moment brief.
The buzzing bee, the fluttering wing,
Small wonders that make our hearts sing.

An unexpected gift, a smile so warm,
In every storm, there's a calm.
The laughter of friends, a shared glance,
In these moments, life finds its dance.

The sound of music, sweet and light,
A candle's flame in the quiet night.
Each heartbeat, a rhythm divine,
Celebrating life, simply benign.

In all the chaos, pause to see,
The small wonders that set us free.
In every day, let gratitude flow,
For the little things that help us grow.

A Map to Inner Sunshine

In the quiet of the morn, I seek,
A golden light where shadows speak.
With each breath, I chart my way,
Through fields of dreams where I can play.

A compass made of hope and cheer,
Guides me gently, year by year.
In heart's embrace, I find my truth,
And walk in joy, rediscover youth.

With every smile, a path is drawn,
Through valleys lush, to break of dawn.
I follow streams of laughter bright,
Creating maps of pure delight.

So when the clouds begin to loom,
I'll hold my light, dispel the gloom.
For in my soul, the stars align,
I've found my way, my inner shine.

Tides of Laughter

Waves of joy crash on the shore,
Each giggle echoes, wanting more.
In the dance of the ocean's song,
I find a place where I belong.

With friends beside, we splash and play,
In sunlight's glow, we seize the day.
The rhythm of our laughter swells,
A melody that time compels.

From the depths, our spirits rise,
Beneath the wide and endless skies.
These tides of joy, we ride with glee,
In every moment, wild and free.

As moonlight bathes the sea so bright,
Our laughter sparkles in the night.
With hearts unbound, we'll always find,
The waves of joy and peace entwined.

The Symphony of Simple Pleasures

In morning's light, I hear the song,
Of birds that chirp the whole day long.
A whisper soft, the breeze does play,
With leaves that dance in a gentle sway.

A fragrant cup of warmth in hand,
Each sip, a treasure, sweetly planned.
The world slows down, I take a breath,
In moments small, I find my wealth.

The laughter shared, the smiles exchanged,
In every hug, love is arranged.
These simple threads weave joy's embrace,
Creating peace, a sacred space.

And when the day draws to a close,
I cherish all, the highs and lows.
In this symphony, I find my joy,
In life's sweet dance, I'm just a boy.

Dancing with Delight

With every step, my spirit flies,
In twirls of joy beneath the skies.
The rhythm flows through heart and vein,
In this embrace, there's no more pain.

With laughter as my guiding tune,
I sway beneath the silver moon.
In every spin, I shed my fears,
The dance of life, through all the years.

As music wraps around my soul,
In joyful leaps, I feel whole.
The world's a stage, and I'm the light,
Embracing dreams, I dance with might.

So let the music play tonight,
And fill the air with pure delight.
In every movement, love ignites,
A dance of joy, our hearts take flight.

Trails of Merry Thoughts

On winding paths where footsteps dance,
Joyful echoes take their chance.
With laughter ringing through the trees,
A whispering breeze brings sweet reprieves.

Each turn reveals a hidden cheer,
The heart feels light, the mind is clear.
Sunbeams sprinkle the tranquil way,
In merry thoughts, we choose to stay.

A flutter of wings in the sky so bright,
Guides us gently into the light.
With every step, our spirits soar,
This trail of joy, we can't ignore.

Let's wander far where dreams reside,
With every thought, our hopes collide.
Together we journey, hand in hand,
On merry trails, together we stand.

Secrets of a Grateful Heart

In the quiet folds of daily life,
A grateful heart cuts through the strife.
In moments small, the treasures bloom,
In simple joys, dispelling gloom.

From sunrise's warmth to evening's sigh,
Every breath is a reason to try.
The gentle rain, the starry night,
In every shadow, there's a light.

Appreciation weaves a gentle thread,
Binding each moment, making us fed.
With open arms, we embrace our fate,
Finding beauty in love's estate.

Let thankfulness echo in every part,
An anthem sung by a grateful heart.
With each note, our spirits rise,
In secrets held, true joy lies.

The Recipe for Laughter

A dash of joy, a sprinkle of fun,
A hearty mix when day is done.
With friends around and spirits high,
Laughter bubbles, catching the eye.

A pinch of whimsy, a wink, a smile,
Stirred together, it's worth the while.
When troubles fade and worries lift,
The gift of laughter's a precious gift.

The recipe's simple, the taste divine,
In every chuckle, the stars align.
With kindness served and warmth as the base,
Laughter's the magic that we embrace.

So gather close, let troubles depart,
Mix love with joy and laughter will start.
With every giggle, our spirits soar,
The recipe for laughter we can't ignore.

Basking in Optimistic Sunlight

With every dawn, the world awakes,
A canvas bright, the heart it makes.
In gentle rays, we find our place,
Basking in the sun's warm embrace.

The shadows fade, worries grow small,
As hope ignites, we stand tall.
Dreams shimmer like the morning dew,
In optimistic light, we find what's true.

Let positivity guide our days,
In every challenge, a hopeful gaze.
With every smile, we weave our fate,
Embracing joy, we celebrate.

So lift your gaze, let troubles fly,
In sunlight's glow, we learn to fly.
Together basking in life's delight,
With hearts aglow, we shine so bright.

Cultivating Blissful Habitats

In fields of green where wildflowers play,
The sun casts shadows in a gentle sway.
Birds sing sweetly in the warm sunlight,
Creating havens, both calm and bright.

With every seed that finds the earth's embrace,
We nurture dreams in this tranquil space.
Water flows softly, whispering peace,
In this world of wonder, all troubles cease.

Together we grow, hearts intertwined,
In harmony's dance, our souls aligned.
The beauty around us, like a timeless song,
In this blissful habitat, we belong.

As twilight descends, stars begin to twinkle,
In the garden's stillness, our hearts mingle.
Under the moon's watchful, silver gaze,
We find joy in life's gentle maze.

Doodles of Delight

Crayons scribbling in colors so bright,
A canvas of dreams captured in light.
Smiles on paper, laughter takes flight,
In a world created, pure and right.

Shapes and lines dance under small hands,
Imagination draws new lands.
Each stroke a story, a magical flight,
Doodles of delight, a child's pure sight.

From whimsical creatures to castles grand,
In every corner, dreams make their stand.
Frames of laughter, moments to share,
In this art of joy, love fills the air.

As colors blend and stories unfold,
These doodles of delight are treasures to hold.
In each little masterpiece, hearts intertwine,
A world made of wonder, endlessly divine.

Harvesting Joyful Moments

In the golden fields where the sunbeams spill,
We gather the laughter, we gather the thrill.
Each grain a memory, each fruit a cheer,
Harvesting moments that we hold dear.

Baskets overflow with the day's sweet grace,
Time spent together in this special place.
Roots intertwined like stories we've shared,
In the heart's rich soil, love has been bared.

As twilight approaches, the colors fade,
We pause to savor the joys we've made.
Every smile collected, each hug and glance,
In this harvest of life, we find our dance.

With every sunset bringing day's end,
We cherish the moments, around us they blend.
Joyful memories, a bountiful treasure,
In the tapestry of life, stitched with pleasure.

Whirlwind of Exuberance

In the dance of the wind, laughter takes flight,
A whirlwind of joy, a heart feeling right.
Spinning and twirling through shades of the day,
In the exuberance, worries drift away.

With every quick step, we chase the sun's glow,
Boundless enthusiasm begins to grow.
The world around us is vibrant and free,
In this joyous tempest, just you and me.

Colors explode like fireworks in the sky,
Moments of bliss as we effortlessly fly.
In the embrace of the storm, we are found,
Our spirits uplifted, joy knows no bound.

As day turns to night, the stars start to gleam,
In this whirlwind of life, we savor the dream.
Together we laugh, together we soar,
In this exhilarating ride, we always want more.

Steps to a Radiant Heart

In quiet moments, breathe in deep,
Let each heartbeat awaken the sleep.
With kindness woven through each thought,
A radiant heart is dearly sought.

Beneath the layers, the light will shine,
Compassion sparks, a love divine.
With every step, let joy impart,
The gentle glow of a radiant heart.

In the embrace of nature's grace,
Find your haven, your sacred place.
As laughter dances, shadows depart,
Revealing the glow of a radiant heart.

Through trials faced, let strength soar high,
In moments still, let spirits fly.
With open arms, receive the art,
Of living fully, a radiant heart.

The Art of Cherishing Moments

In fleeting seconds, life unfolds,
A treasure trove, a tale retold.
With every glance, hold close and near,
The beauty found in laughter, cheer.

As sunbeams kiss the morning dew,
Each moment whispers, fresh and new.
In simple joys, let hearts ignite,
The art of cherishing feels so right.

From tiny blooms to skies so wide,
In each heartbeat, let love abide.
Embrace the now, let worries fade,
In the warmth of gratitude, be swayed.

With every story that fills the air,
Let joy be woven in each prayer.
The art of cherishing brings delight,
A canvas painted with pure light.

Finding Delight in the Ordinary

In morning coffee, warmth aglow,
In rustling leaves, where soft winds blow.
In every moment, a gem may hide,
Finding delight, our hearts abide.

A child's laughter, pure and sweet,
In mundane tasks, life's rhythm beats.
The flicker of candles, the moon's embrace,
In ordinary life, we find our place.

The gentle rain, a soothing sound,
In quiet corners, joy is found.
With open eyes, let wonder start,
Finding delight in the simplest art.

In whispers of love, in friendships dear,
In soft goodnights, in every tear.
Ordinary moments, treasures unfold,
In every heart, a story told.

Blooming in Unexpected Places

In cracks of pavement, blooms arise,
Against the odds, they touch the skies.
Resilience taught by nature's hand,
A lesson deep, we understand.

With colors bright where shadows creep,
In hearts once weary, dreams can leap.
A hopeful bud, a fragrant grace,
Blooming forth in unexpected space.

Through storms that ravage, through night's dark song,
Life finds a way to carry on.
From ashes rise, new paths begin,
In every struggle, strength within.

So let your spirit, like flowers, grow,
In every challenge, let love flow.
For even in the tough and rough,
Blooming in life is just enough.

Milton Keynes UK
Ingram Content Group UK Ltd.
UKHW051811101024
449294UK00007BA/55

9 789916 882443